Memories Evoked

Batter Bowl to the Battlefield

by Carol Jean Estes

All photography by Carol Estes

(except where noted)

Welcome to Carol World, Inc. 2016

This life is quite a journey.
We have all taken an oar in
hand at some point, leaned in
and paddled forward.

Without memories, our voyages
would be far less engaging.
Right or wrong, good or bad,
memories make us stronger,
and hopefully better people.

I hope something touches you,
and helps reinforce the fact that
we do not journey alone.

Dunescape

Table of Contents

Girl with blue bucket

Memories Forged

As photographers, we create, react to, and sustain memories with each click of the camera.

Big Gear, Big Sky

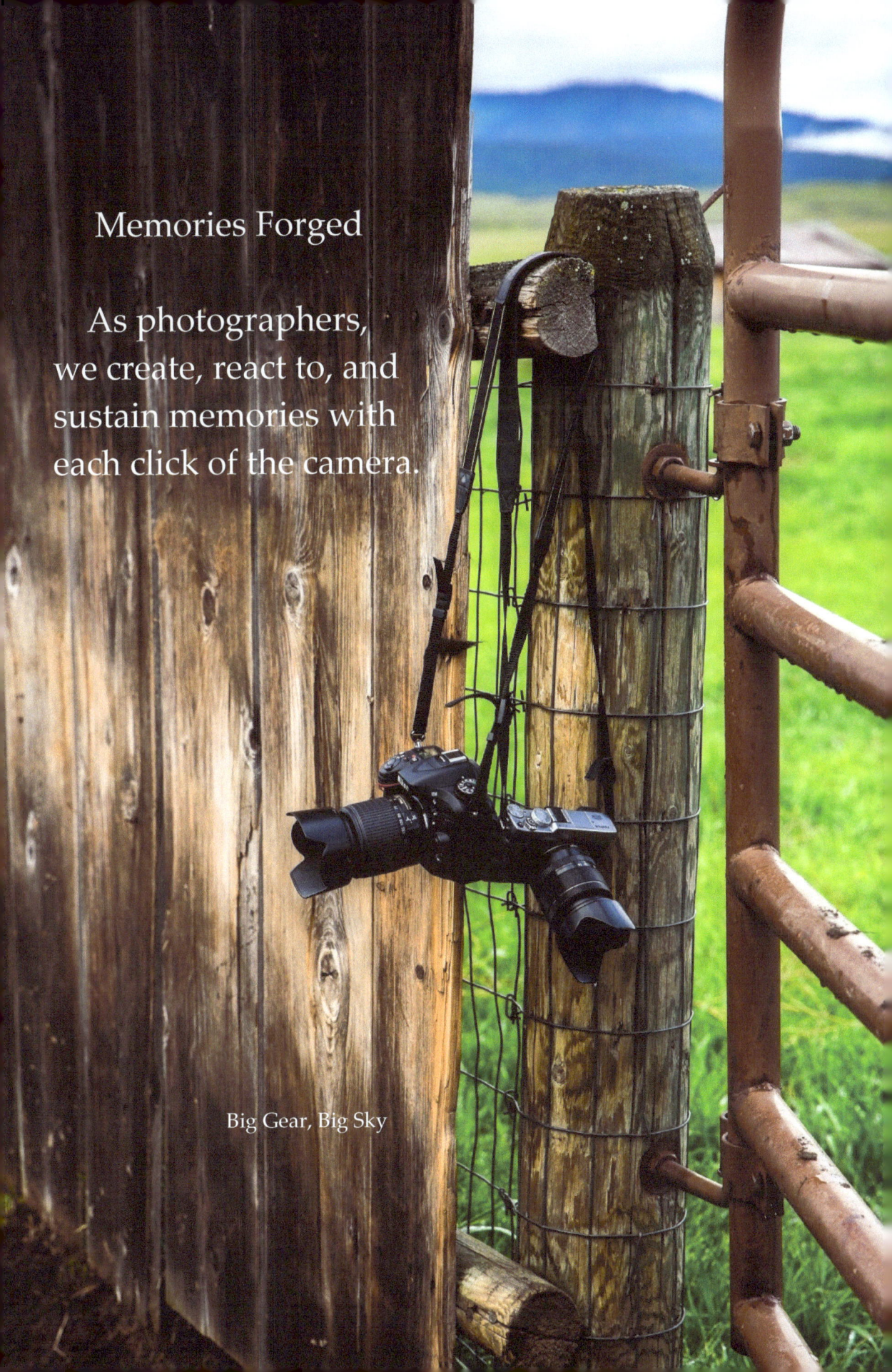

Steve Bensing

I trace my love for photography back to my grandfather, Robert Reese.

Grandpa was a Feed Salesman by trade, but he had a passion for photography.

As a young child, I was fascinated by a mysterious place in his basement that he used as a darkroom. I was mesmerized by the magic of a picture appearing in a tray of liquid under a strange-colored light. I still have his enlarger, an Omega D II, which is now in my own darkroom.

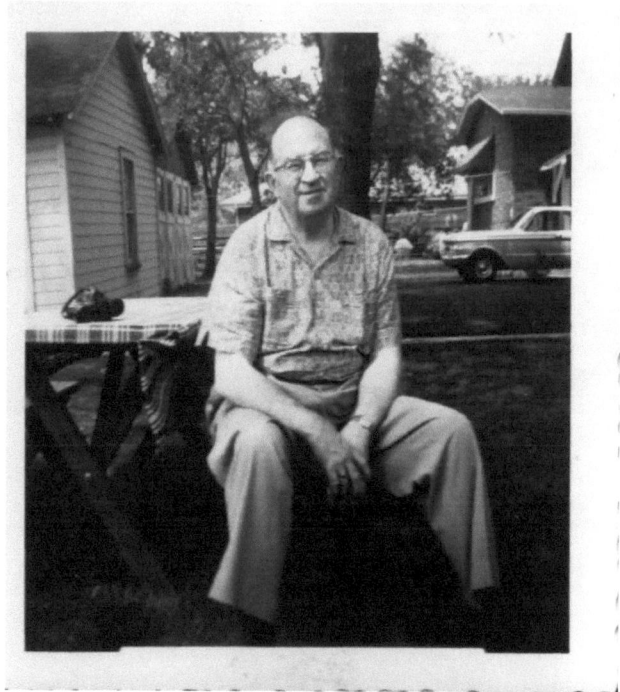

courtesy of Steven Bensing

This photo is the first one I remember taking with my first camera, a Savoy plastic box camera, which used 620 film that produced twelve 2 ¼ x 2 ¼ inch negatives on a roll. The low angle of the image was from the perspective of a five-year-old child. When Grandpa was seated, he was more at my level. I snapped the photo in his yard in Harvey, IL.

A Corvair from the early 1960's, in the neighbor's driveway, gives a sense of time to the picture. Besides Grandpa, there are a couple of other items of significance in this photograph. He is sitting at a redwood picnic table, which is a little worse for the wear, but currently resides in my backyard. On that table is a camera in a case, my Grandpa's Leica IIIf, which he purchased in the early 1950's. That Leica became the first 35mm camera I used when I took photography classes at Waukegan High School. Years later when my son, Silas, was taking high school photography, he learned with the same camera. He's grown now, but still has that Leica, and shoots black and white film with it in New York.

This photo for me, represents the first link in a chain of the love of photography. Through the generations, that memory lives on.

Rhonda Mullen

My Dad
Sheldon E Simon

courtesy of Rhonda Mullen

This photo was taken in 1980 by my Dad, Sheldon Simon.

He was a steel man by necessity, and a photographer by heart.

We would spend weeks at a time traveling the country taking photos.

Yellowstone was one of his favorite spots. In 2016, I took Mia, my granddaughter, now nearly seven, on a pilgrimage. We visited some of Dad's favorite places, saying "Hello, Dad" at every stop. Mia and I compiled our own photo journals from this journey, our memories treasured.

Henry Schultz

I re-ignited my interest in photography in 2010, after giving up the old Pentax 35mm in 1975.

The dark room was replaced with digital files, photo processing, apps, and my Nikon.

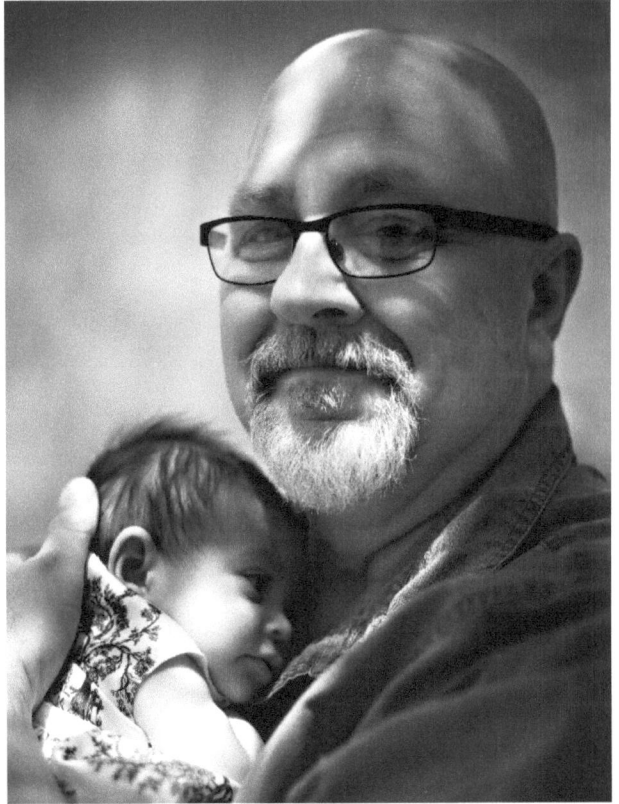

courtesy of Henry Schultz

I started out shooting nature, but became more geared to Fine Art Photography.

In a continuing quest, honing my skills in portrait work, I found my way to make magic happen, using light. This image is my precious four-month-old niece, Braylin and myself. The magic of life, the magic of light, and oh, how it makes us smile.

Carol Estes

My journey with music has been life-long. My father was a music teacher and musician.

I practiced years in school with my flute, and his musical compass instilled an affection nothing else can match.

courtesy of
Mark Biegel

Life's bumpy road brought me together with a camera, into the company of the Biegel brothers. After 25 years, in swing bands, life separated the brothers by design and schedules. One night, these twin brothers found their way before my camera lens. A moment of pure chance to "reframe yesterday".

"Twinning", Mark and John Biegel
by Carol Estes

La Familia

The term family is very broad.
And we find how deep
our roots can reach,
with friends and neighbors.

Turn Key

"Her Last Day"
by Robin Janota

The painting is called "Her Last Day" and was inspired by my career at Ford Motor Company.

Ford was my life for 20 years.

Leaving to move out west and take care of my terminally ill Mother, was the scariest thing I ever did.

The expression on the face in the painting signifies the fear, but also the determination and pride in having been a Toolmaker.

Original painting by Robin Janota

The light switch signifies the change from one part of life to the next. The glow of light around her is pure power, divine energy that is with us all.

"Missouri Minutes"
by Carol Estes

Stacking the dishes in the cabinet, I ran my thumb and finger around the turquoise ring of Grandma's Anchor Hocking cups. I wasn't a coffee drinker yet, but I loved to stack away her cups and saucers. There was always a lot of chatter in Grandma's kitchen. Dish cloths in hands, the dishes rattled in the plastic tub. Just inches of soapy water were kept in the sink, so the sistern did not run dry.

Out the back screen lay the big flat rocks by the water pump. Remembering that spring afternoon, tripping, as my cousin rode piggyback. Compound broken arm, age nine. Mom and the Aunts ran screaming out of the kitchen. Grandma to the rescue.

The heavy cast is now cumbersome after three months.

Turning to the voices in the other doorway, I spy the infamous pump organ. Hours of fun, with a limit of palatable music. But I was always drawn to the nine-panel glass French doors.

The "north room" was always closed. On rare occasions we were granted a "touch and feel journey" through glassware and porcelain gleaming with fanciful designs. The elegance of it all. Stacked and displayed, a trove of treasure.

To one in my pre-tweens, it was all magic. Glistening facets I perceived serving opulent table settings. A Missouri homestead transformed into a royal banquet.

It's late August now, the cast is itchy, and the light starts to fade in the north room. Outside the music begins. The cicadas raise up a chorus of harmonies, their fervor of life like no other.

Collecting their hard shells off the trees in Grandma's yard is just a given activity. I think my personal daily best was twenty-two. For this city girl, there was no greater joy than summer in Northwest Missouri.

The Dekalb County Record, the local newspaper would royally proclaim next week, "Velma's granddaughter Carol Jean of Kansas City came to visit". She always called me Carol Jean. The party line, was she one long and two shorts? I could never remember. We counted the local population one night on the porch swing. There were fifty-two, well, if you count Uncle Pedro's farm out east, and the Sandgren cousins and their peacocks out west.

There was plenty of fishing. And, I would always check the stash of Pepsi in tall bottles at Aunt Frieda's, an exceptional treat. The whoosh from the cap when lifted, and the taste, a manna from heaven.

The center of town, my playground, was just a four way stop. Aunt Rosalie had the general store on the corner. At the kitty-corner were the restaurant and post office.

Across the road, Max Neil's regulars taught me to play spit, a card game, in his greasy gas station. I am sure I drove him crazy, jumping accidently, of course on the air hose that rang the bell in front of the pumps.

I lived a life in a week. I crawled into the hay barn, collected eggs, and watched cousins on horseback at the 4-H County Fair.

I giggled at the name of the "naked ladies" a beautifully fragrant lily that sprang from the ground with no foliage.

Grandma had a chronically bad back. The visiting grandkids shared her bed tipped up at the headboard, with a large plank under the weathered mattress for extra support. Grandma's snoring, infamous as it was, could out-sing a chain saw. But, remember, this comes from a nine-year-old, full of fanciful tales.

Coney Island

Grandma lived most of her 92 years two doors down from Max Neil's station, with the bank in between. Her beautiful flower garden is now their drive-thru window. Each end of town flanked by the First Baptist Church at one end, and by the Methodist Church at the other. Behind the Methodist sanctuary, is the cemetery where my family is buried. So many miles from then to now.

Today, I stand out front of the cemetery gate. The view unchanged in nearly 50 years, still stands the weight of time. Mom and Dad returned here to live out that time, where so many memories were created.

My camera in hand, its vivid stills pale to the slideshow of my youth. Snapshots of reunions, weddings, funerals, and my week with Grandma. I spent over a quarter of a century finding new homes for beautiful antique china and cut glass. Grandma would have surely approved. I don't know where her turquoise dishes were taken, or whether anyone else retained such a tender thought from them. My kitchen is now filled to the brim with every turquoise kitchen gadget, a fleeting connection at Grandma's.

Life has become a continuous loop of Missouri minutes.

Knit One, Pearl's Two
by Carol Estes

When you look thru the sewing machine, you see "Cupid Awake". It is one of a series of vintage images my mother so revered. In the turn of the last century, Josephine Anderson, a lovely four-year-old, had the good fortune to meet up with local photographer M.B. Parkinson.

Knit One, Pearl's Two

Parkinson, posed the young neighbor as her model, and created the "Cupid Awake" and "Cupid Asleep" series. It has been popular since its release about 1897. This is Mom's copy, that hung in our home for years. I collected the other items from my antique store, to tell a new story. A friend reminded me that I misspelled, "Purl", the correct action in knitting. It is all a play on words.

Mom loved to sew, and made much of our clothing, even up thru high school. Her idea of a hemline in 1972, was two inches below the knee. She tried to teach me, but this southpaw had a left brain fail. I could do elastic waistbands, but never could master buttonholes and zippers. In my closet, I still have a Japanese inspired kimono jacket. Mom created it, when I was twenty-five, for an important date in the early 1980's with my eventual husband.

As it turned out, my love of antiques, created the biggest bridge between my Mom and myself. She so enjoyed digging thru boxes at auctions, and waiting hours for her special purchases. Even when dementia started to seep thru the cracks, we could talk vintage and the like, and her eyes would perk up. That light extinguished in 2005, at 82 years of age.

Billie is 90

A slight little china doll,
Billie is 90.
a product of life's frailties.
Broken, but not forgotten

The world passes
like the speed of light.
Yet, she peers out the window
as if time has stopped.

Rain taps on the rooftop
The twinkle in her eyes dim slightly.
A forward lean, fragile hands
gracefully folded one over the other.

Lips pursed, a quick sigh.
Shoulders rise up and back,
as her breath gently retreats.

Those hazel eyes meet yours.
An air of resignation.,
This is her September song.

But, in a flash she returns.
Her tipping glance slides back
to those who hold her dear.

The love wells up, she smiles.
A snapshot of mere perfection.
There's never a way to say goodbye.

Just thank you. Billie is 90.

The State of Things

Indiana: 1816-2016

A slippery slope!

Our Hoosier Heart
by Carol Estes

Our call of the Cardinal,
life pairs unite,
carry chronicles of yore.
With nesting generations,
seasons change,
la familia flourishes.

Our Hoosier Heart thrives.

Enter War and Hate,
North and South,
kindred spirits opposed.
Powder horns packed,
Father and Brother compelled,
Mother and Wife resigned.

Our Hoosier Heart bleeds

Challenged and rewarded,
Tested and resilient
yet, intolerance evolves.
Scars of Sojourner,
Hate stitched in white,
A pointed cloth degrades.

Our Hoosier Heart Ashamed

Hark scarlet wings
The sounds of spring
nest we bind and weave.
Now, two hundred years.
torches held high,
our world we now avow.

Our Hoosier Heart Heals

On wings of progress,
crossroads we motto.
We play, we work, we vote.

Our Hoosier Heart now beats with Pride.

Bless our Hoosier Heart!

It's a long, hard road!

Juxtaposition

A Dream in Repose

As my home for over 30 years,

Plein Lane

my adopted state is a symphony of space and color.

1875 Covered Bridge built by JJ Daniels
photo taken after the flood of the
White River July, 2015 Medora, Indiana

Courtesy of Robin Janota

LaPorte County, IN

Watercolors
by Carol Estes

An American Quilt

Weary Travel

For Old Glory

Shepherd, by Proxy

Shepherd, by Proxy

by Carol Estes

My grid of stars hold steady
a catalyst of speech,
voices cry in factious debate.
Here I am, Here I stand!

Soft are ripples off the breeze,
the snap and swivel doth chime.
Quiet as it seems to be,
yet my tenor not at ease.

Pantone colors, paints to revere
the weathered stripes ensue.
Tattered crimson now does pale
yet, my rugged cloth shall hale.

I weep the souls that cross me.
I bleed to those that fight me.
Foul vein of hate, their words abate.
Here I am, Here I stand!

Memorial Day Salute, American Legion Post 83 LaPorte, IN

Flag Code of America

based on Title 4 of the National Flag Code of June 14, 1923

- The flag should be lighted at all times, either by sunlight or by an appropriate light source.
- The flag should be flown in fair weather, unless the flag is designed for inclement weather use.
- The flag should never be dipped to any person or thing. It is flown upside down only as a distress signal.
- The flag should not be used for any decoration in general. Bunting of blue, white and red stripes is available for these purposes. The blue stripe of the bunting should be on the top.
- The flag should never be used for any advertising purpose. It should not be embroidered, printed or otherwise impressed on such articles as cushions, handkerchiefs, napkins, boxes, or anything intended to be discarded after temporary use. Advertising signs should not be attached to the staff or halyard.
- The flag should not be used as part of a costume or athletic uniform, except that a flag patch may be used on the uniform of military personnel, fireman, policeman and members of patriotic organizations.
- The flag should never have any mark, insignia, letter, word, number, figure, or drawing of any kind placed on it, or attached to it
- The flag should never be used for receiving, holding, carrying, or delivering anything.
- When the flag is lowered, no part of it should touch the ground or any other object; it should be received by waiting hands and arms. To store the flag it should be folded neatly and ceremoniously.

- The Flag should be cleaned and mended when necessary.
- When a flag is so worn it is no longer fit to serve as a symbol of our country, it should be destroyed by burning in a dignified manner.

Flag Disposal Ceremony, VFW Indiana Post 1130, LaPorte, Indiana (June 2016)

Thank you for your Service!

Aftermath

Civil War Hospital, Indiana 9th Regiment, LaPorte, IN

You Don't Look Back

by Carol Estes

Over your shoulder, the landscape is paved.
Boots and epaulettes worn thru.
Bittersweet are the fruits of labor.

Your politics unwavering, voice of speech,
Rights we cherish on a platter of faith.
Youth renewed, and a sense of entitlement.

Yet, you don't look back.

A lottery ticket for one. No girls to court, or engines retuned
Uncle Sam points with fervor. "You are the answer".
Dreams dashed, white collar and tie stowed.
He trained, he transported, sacrificed his youth.
But, the rains came. An invisible, insidious falling.
War goes back on its heels, now suffer the soldiers.
An agent like no other, expose, deny, is their reply.
Forward to the farm he once knew, now chasing answers,
crippling anatomy. Signs of trouble, rejections,
pleas for help. Decades for vindication.

The Naval Recruit, hedging the draft.
A newlywed, a rascal of sorts.
Ports of call, gambling debts,
and sanity saved by Tolkien's World.
A lucky sailor who found his way unscathed.
But, was he?

A boy with friends, a bevy for life, the call for action surfaces.
An inner voice, calling "Be All You Can Be".
The young recruit finds structure, trust, and loyalty.
While the bevy circles the fire pit,
bottoms out Cherry Dip Road.

Tours on a carrier, deployed in the jungle,
but the mind tangles in the undergrowth.
Homeward bound, the military spirits vanish,
The bevy now strangers, searching for the new normal.
Anxiety pressed inward, a silent curse, medications wasted.
PTSD tossed about, but true answers escape.

The Junior Cadet, not yet of age, with a true call for duty.
Training in the sky, service tours abroad.
The Ranger hears the Sands of the Desert stir.
Deep in maneuvers, boots on the ground, pulled on special leave.
Tears run to bury his mother. More life sacrificed for service.

A chill in the affairs of state, tho' reference for democracy ensues.
Services of Veterans and Actives run generation to generation.
They cringed the mockery, but protected those who speak,
raised arms so you can strike the flag.

Thousands fought so you may dishonor the fallen.
We fight, to agree to disagree.
Our circle of life, is a circle of freedom.

This story has no ending.
The trenches are not empty,
the storm of dissent may never calm.

Stop, now!

Look back, and know that you stand now in your shadow,
by virtue of the shadows that fell before you.

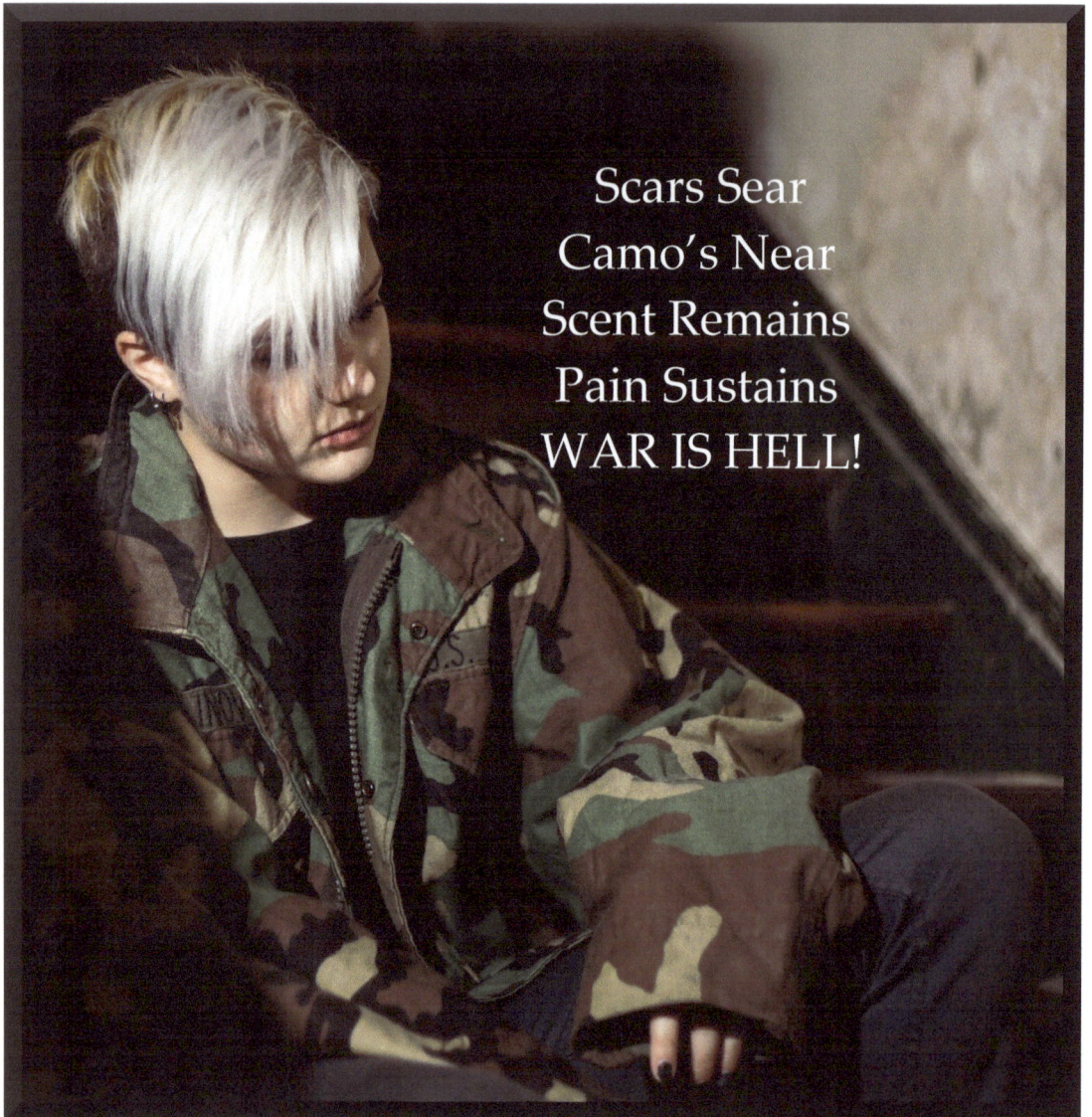

Scars Sear
Camo's Near
Scent Remains
Pain Sustains
WAR IS HELL!

"Ruminations"
Hannah Thompson

Honor Guard

A Widow at War

by Carol Estes

Paralyzed, without hope, the outbound train
is enveloped by the horizon.
Drawn back to timetables, a creaking platform,
as the clock stands still.

My feet are now weighted before my dispatch,
seeking resolution.
The flickering light, dimmed day by day,
of news to repair my soul.

I now wake to a vast wasted space.
I now eat to a vast wasted space.
I cry for you, in the shroud of the vast wasted space.

I look for who has robbed you,
of your freedom, your self, your breath.
Only clues, scrabble board tilts, the puzzle lays dormant.
Wires broken, causeways breeched, lives unfinished.

All that surfaces is HATE.
Yes, you are HATE,
evil as the torment of Revelations.
Only, upon return, you reap havoc,
and the ruination of humanity.

You are HATE,
evil as the eye of Mephistopheles,
raising his tankard.

You are HATE, a coward dressed
under auspices of a cause
You trick those seeking purpose,
and sacrifice your youth
Yet enroll the services of others,
while hiding to save yourself.

Visions now in the eyes of my child,
whose questions never cease.
Why does that man have no eye, Momma?
Why does that woman have no legs, Momma?
It scares me!

How do I explain the ruthlessness of HATE?
How do I instill there is goodness in mankind?
You are HATE, shredding all I know is wise.

You are HATE, but, you will not triumph,
and I will not concede.
Forced now to journey alone,
I assemble weapons of peace and humility.
But first, I must celebrate this Flag-draped box,

MY AMERICAN DREAM.

The Invisible Men
by Carol Estes

The silence in their lives is untenable.
They push, pull or carry their life's possessions.
They have walked every street,
yet they are the Invisible Men.

Lives complicated by combat, alcohol,
and the mind robbing them of center,
balance, and ability.
Those around look, but do not see.

Many have found unity on the train.
A camaraderie of sorts, no judgments,
and the hope of peace.
Seizing an open door, their clamoring entrance
echoes in the empty car.
Back and forth, North and South
To the world and beyond.
From Duluth to the Big Easy,
The Invisible men ride long and hard.

We know not what they seek.

Perhaps, because no one asked.

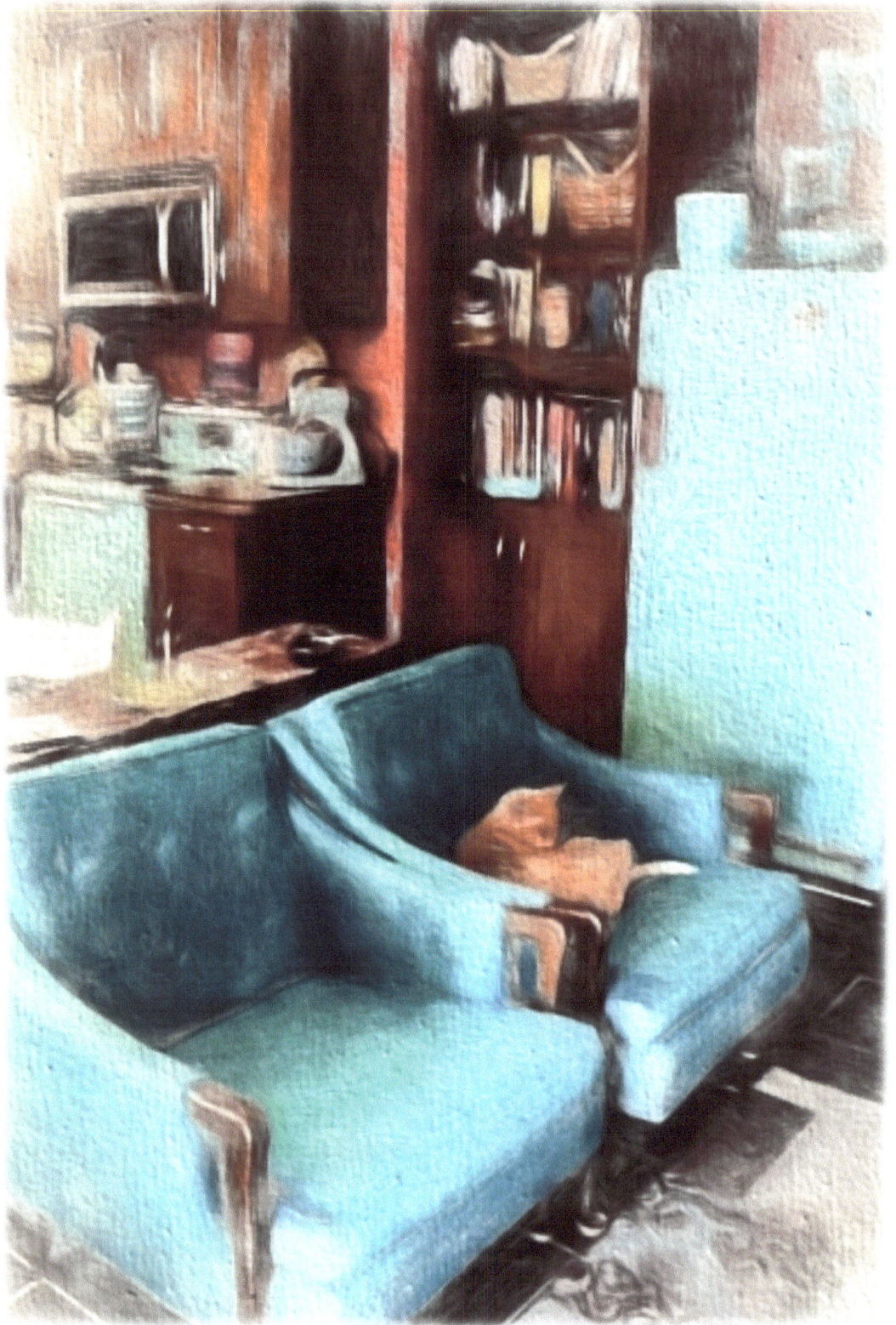

Modus Operandi

(Ingredients for recipes of life)

Memories and the connection with food is universal. I've had so many great conversations, intellectual repartee, and laughter until you cry as I shared food and drink with friends and loved ones. The tradition and structure of family meal time has carried down thru the generations. All family gatherings, reunions, and memorial meals started with the pleasure of company, and saying grace. I think I was lucky to learn what table conversation can glean.

I enjoyed making Grandmother's Special Filled Cookies before we would go visit. Grandma would tell me, I made the best cookies from her recipe. I would share my fruit preserves, cobblers and apple butter. There are great rewards from the connection that food elicits, as the circle completes.

Summer bounty in Northwest Missouri was a high point, with corn on the cob by the bushel basket, fresh berries, and green beans to snap until your fingers hurt. My parents found local community gardens close to home, where we planted, weeded, and harvested. We also traveled to local farms and orchards, climbed ladders to pick plums, apples, and peaches. I learned to prep, can, and freeze all sorts of luscious summer favorites.

Grandmother's Filled Cookies

Sugar cookie

2 ¼ c. flour
1 ½ tsp baking powder
¼ tsp salt
1 ½ tsp lemon or vanilla
½ cup butter or margarine
1 c. sugar
2 eggs well beaten
1 Tbsp. milk

Beat eggs, butter and sugar.
Add flour, dry ingredients extract and milk.
Refrigerate for at least two hours.
Roll out thin, on lightly floured
surface and cut out flat rounds.

Filling

2 c. choice of raisins
2 c. orange juice

Simmer for 10 minutes, and set aside.

Stir in

2 c. chopped nuts
(I prefer Missouri Pecans)
¼ c. brown sugar
1 Tbsp. corn starch
(adjust for thickness)

Place small dab of filling in the center, and layer
another sugar round on top. Lightly press around
the edges. Bake in a 350 degree oven for 6-8 minutes,
or until edges are lightly brown. Time will vary by oven.
Remove and cool.

Fruit Cobbler

½ stick butter
½ c. flour
½ c. sugar
½ c. milk
1 tsp baking powder
1 ½ to 2 cups fresh or frozen blackberries or raspberries,
sweetened to taste.

Melt butter until it starts to brown. Pour into 1 ½ quart baking
dish. Mix flour, sugar, baking powder and milk. Pour over
melted butter. Spread sweetened fruit over melted butter and
batter. Bake about 30 minutes in a 375 degree oven. Serves 4-6.
Best while still slightly warm topped with whipped cream.

My Father was a teacher, and Mom had jobs that kept her until
after 5pm. The dining room table was our meeting place. We
always had two meals together each day, Breakfast and Dinner.
There were no accessories allowed. We only had one phone on
a cord to the wall, and the newspapers were delivered twice each
day. At the table no phone calls could be taken. Saturday dinner,
was the exception for television during the meal. Well, of course,
we couldn't miss Jackie Gleason and the June Taylor Dancers.

I wasn't a highly social child, outside of school and church. I would hang with Mom and Dad on Saturday night. Some fall nights, I would get peckish, and hit the kitchen for perhaps, cold fried chicken and hot tea. I would return with fresh Apple Sauce Doughnuts. Well, it just sounded good.

Apple Sauce Doughnuts

3 ⅓ c. flour divided
1 Tbsp. baking powder
½ tsp salt
¾ tsp cinnamon
¼ tsp cloves (if desired)
1 c. apple sauce (homemade is best)
¾ c. sugar
2 eggs
2 Tbsp. shortening

Put 1⅓ c. flour in bowl. Add next 8 ingredients
Beat at low speed until well mixed.
Increase speed to medium, and beat for 2 minutes.

Stir in remaining flour, cover and chill for 1 hour.

Divide dough in half, and roll each to ½ inch thick.

Cut and fry in 2-3 inches of hot oil for 1 minute on each side

Drain on paper towel
Roll in cinnamon sugar
or dust with powdered sugar

My father's duty on Saturday night, was to run to Zarda Dairy for any necessaries for breakfast ahead of Sunday Church services. My father's breakfast every day that I could remember, included two slices of bacon, two eggs basted, and Wonder White Bread with sorghum. He never toasted.

At 10 o'clock, he would catch a bit of the news, and head out, fill my Mother's car with gasoline, and return with either Black Walnut or Butter Pecan Ice Cream.

The kitchen was one of my favorite places in the house. Especially, when we moved the little 13 inch black and white television to the top of the dishwasher. Cooking, and family recipes became very important.

Parsnips ready for roasting

Life is full of ups and downs, love and loss. The world is a plethora of culture, and their foods can bring together minds and bodies. We break bread for celebrating, mourning, and sometimes for therapy. The people we meet, can stay with us forever. It was fate that a Sushi night brought two grieving wives together, to help each other heal. But, for the fact of that meeting, nearly 10 years ago, we would not have grown to our full potential today.

思考の糧
Shikō no kate
Food for Thought

Memories Evoked
an amalgam of life.
Treasure what you have,
and protect what you know.

Dedication

A late winter night in January 2013, I walked into Paul Henry's Art Gallery, in Hammond, Indiana.

With crockpot in hand, I introduced myself to David Mueller. He asked me if I was an artist. As a very green photographer, I told him, "I take pictures". (At the time, that was the truth).

From there, my life's journey was hitched to the weekly Acoustic Jam/Open Table Potluck on Thursday nights. It was there that I had my first opportunity to perform Spoken Word, and share as a new writer. I am now fortunate to be an integral part of the Art Gallery, as a poet and a photographer.

One night, after reading a new piece, I felt a tap on my shoulder. There was a voice in my ear. "I want a copy of your first book." I turned in astonishment, and there sat Mary LeVan, a soldier and cheerleader to all those she can touch. Now at 87, I say thank you, Mary LeVan. We all want to be like you when we grow up.

And, nothing on these pages would have come to fruition without the support of David and Rita Mueller, the Gallery owners. Local artists in NW Indiana, have been so lucky to walk thru your door, watch your heart and drive to give us a place to shine.

Contributors

I have to say a special thank you to those that helped me put this project together.

<u>Photographer Stories</u>

Steve Bensing
Northern Light Images
Valparaiso, IN

Rhonda Mullen
Whispered Photography
Portage, IN

Henry Schultz
Henry Schultz Photography
Portage, IN

Robin Janota
Robin Red Feather Original Art LLC
Valparaiso, IN

The continued service of the
Veterans of Foreign Wars Post 1130
American Legion Post 83
LaPorte County, IN

And the contributions of friends and family.

IN MEMORIAM

Life draws you to some unexpected junctures.

Last winter I listened to an inner voice that compelled me to create a small book on memories, that upheld my belief in people, the flag, and our country.

I was put on a track to attend several events with the Honor Guard of the American Legion Post 83 of LaPorte, Indiana. Today, a friend invited me to a regular gathering at the Post. In conversation, he happened to mention the Sargent of the Guard, Leon Hubner, had passed away unexpectedly just hours before.

I had only met Leon a couple of times, but had seen his stalwart salute nearly every day since June, as I compiled this personal piece. It was an emotional moment, to realize my book on memories had become a memory all its own.

So, just days before this book is published, we lose another servant to the world.

Salute, Leon, and thank you for your service.

October 1, 2016

About the Author

Carol Estes is an Art photographer, and writer of poetry and prose. In 2006, Carol experienced several traumatic events. In order to heal
and grieve, picked up a digital camera and started writing. These creative ventures altered her journey, hence the phrase "Welcome to
Carol World...life as I see it!"

An award winning photographer, Carol was also selected to the 2014 Hoosier Women's Artists. She has exhibited in Juried Shows and Art Galleries in Missouri, Michigan, Illinois, andIndiana. Carol has also been published in numerous magazines with her portrait art photographs.

Performance Art is also part of Carol's repertoire. Carol has appeared on local stages in Indiana and Michigan, and on the historic stage of The Green Mill, in Chicago, Illinois.

"Memories Evoked" is Carol's first published work. Carol resides in LaPorte, IN.

www.welcometocarolworld.com

www.ingramcontent.com/pod-product-compliance
Lightning Source LLC
Chambersburg PA
CBHW041426090426
42741CB00002B/48